Getting To Know...

Nature's Children

WOLVES

Judy Ross

SCHOLASTIC INC.

New York Toronto London Auckland Sydney
Mexico City New Delhi Hong Kong Buenos Aires

Facts in Brief

Classification of the wolf

    Class: *Mammalia* (mammals)

    Order: *Carnivora* (meat-eaters)

    Family: *Canidae* (dog family)

    Genus: *Canis*

    Species: *Canis lupus* (common name is Gray Wolf)

World distribution. Europe, Asia, and North America.

Habitat. Various.

Distinctive physical characteristics. Look very much like German Shepherd dogs except for longer legs, narrower chests, larger feet, and rounded ears; wolves of different regions tend to differ in color.

Habits. Usually live in small, strictly organized packs of related animals; packs mark and defend a territory; the wolves of some areas migrate seasonally.

Diet. Herd animals, birds, and small mammals.

Revised edition copyright © 1996 by Scholastic Inc.
Original material © 1985 Grolier Limited.
All rights reserved.

Published by Scholastic Inc.
90 Old Sherman Turnpike, Danbury, Connecticut 06816.

SCHOLASTIC and associated logos are trademarks of Scholastic Inc.

ISBN 0-7172-6698-2   Printed in the U.S.A.

Edited by: Elizabeth Grace Zuraw   *Photo Editor:* Nancy Norton
Photo Rights: Ivy Images   *Cover Design*: Niemand Design

Have you ever wondered . . .

When you think of a wolf, what comes to mind? The tricky wolf who dressed up like a grandma to fool Little Red Riding Hood? The big bad wolf who blew the Three Little Pigs' house down? Or maybe a thriller movie in which a wolf's long, eerie howl was used in some scary scene to make you cringe and slide down, bulge-eyed, in your seat?

In many stories, cartoons, and other entertainments, wolves are often portrayed as sly and sneaky or just plain mean. No wonder people fear and dislike them.

Because of the wolf's bad reputation, you might be surprised to learn that, like most wild animals, wolves are probably more frightened of us than we are of them. In addition, wolves are beautiful and intelligent animals. Loyal to each other, they live in close family groups and take special care of their young.

Wolves don't deserve the bad name they've gotten. Let's read about them and find out why.

A handsome creature, the wolf is one of the largest members of the dog family.

Roly-Poly Pup

With its soft, fuzzy coat and baby-blue eyes, a young wolf looks a lot like a pet puppy dog. In fact, baby wolves are called *pups*. And like a puppy dog, a wolf pup loves to play with its brothers and sisters.

As the pups tumble over each other, an adult wolf stands guard nearby. If this "babysitter" senses danger, it quickly sends the pups scurrying to the safety of their *den,* or home.

Play teaches the wolf pup many things. Perhaps the most important lesson a pup must learn is its place in its *pack,* or family group. When a pup begins to lose in a play fight, it rolls over on its back, ending the fight. The stronger pup is almost always the winner. It stands with its tail in the air, as if to say, "I am the ruler here!" This is the basic law of a pack—*subordinate,* or weaker, wolves always obey the *dominant,* or stronger, ones.

Before these pups' first birthday, they'll be almost as large as their parents.

Dog Cousins

Wolves are related to coyotes, foxes, jackals, dingos, and to our pet dogs.

Fox

People often get the wolf and its cousin, the coyote, mixed up because they look so much alike. But if you put a wolf and a coyote side by side, you can see that wolves are larger and stockier than coyotes.

The Gray Wolf is the most common kind of wolf. It's the largest wild member of the dog family. The only other true wolf is the Red Wolf, a separate kind of wolf found in the southeastern United States. It's population is very small.

Coyote

Wolf

Gray Wolves that live in forested areas are called Timber Wolves.

Where They Live

Wolves once lived all over North America, but today their range is much smaller. Gray Wolves live mostly in the wild lands of Canada and Alaska and in northern parts of the lower United States, including Minnesota, Wisconsin, Michigan, Montana, Idaho, and Washington. Some wolves prefer to live in forested areas. Others live farther north in the *tundra,* the arctic regions where there are no trees. The forest-dwellers are usually gray to black in color; they are also known as Timber Wolves. The tundra-dwellers are generally lighter in color; they are also known as Tundra Wolves.

Our North American wolves have relatives in Asia, Italy, Scandinavia, Spain, and Portugal, and parts of Eastern Europe.

The Wolf Up Close

You've heard of the Big Bad Wolf, but how big are wolves in real life? Some large males weigh more than 100 pounds (45 kilograms) and are 6 feet (2 meters) from nose to tail tip. But most males are about the size of a German Shepherd dog, and the females are slightly smaller.

Although some wolves look a lot like German Shepherds, they have longer legs and bigger feet than these dog relatives. And their bodies look more streamlined because their chests are narrower.

Wolves come in a wide range of colors. Most are grayish—or mixtures of black, gray, tan, brown, and white that make them look gray. Some are mostly black, while others are white, especially in the far North. Sometimes even wolf pups in the same *litter*— the animals that are born together—have different colors of coats.

Wolf tracks

11

On the Move

Like dogs, wolves run on their toes. This lets them take long strides. For short distances they can run about 34 miles (55 kilometers) an hour. Although that's pretty fast, most of the wolf's *prey,* the animals wolves hunt for food, are even faster. Those that aren't faster can often escape the wolves by zigzagging and turning suddenly. But wolves have one advantage. They are almost tireless and can run for hours.

Most wolves are also amazingly strong and agile. A full-grown wolf can leap as high as a one-story building!

Wolves are genuine long-distance runners. They can go for hours without tiring.

A Big Family

Wolves like company and live in packs. The members of the pack are usually the mother and father and their young, along with aunts, uncles, and cousins. Most wolf packs have 7 or 8 members, but some have 20 or more.

A pack always has a leader, called the *alpha male*. He is usually the strongest male in the group. The *alpha female* is his mate. Every other pack member knows its place and quickly learns to follow the alpha male and alpha female.

Wolf families are affectionate and cooperative. They play and hunt together. They protect each other, too. If one wolf gets into trouble, the others try to help it.

A wolf pack is a close and highly organized family group. Members live, play, travel, and hunt together.

Leader of the Pack

It's easy to tell which wolf is the pack leader. He's usually the biggest. He stands proud and tall with his tail and head held high. He knows that he's in charge. When he approaches another wolf in his pack, it will cower, hang its head down, and put its tail between its legs. Then it'll roll over on its back, as if to say, "I give up—you're too strong for me!" This is why wolves seldom fight among themselves. The weaker ones almost always show proper respect before a real fight breaks out.

Occasionally a wolf lives alone. Usually these are young adults searching for a mate and vacant territory where they can start a pack of their own. Sometimes lone wolves are former leaders that have lost their place in the pack.

The pack leader often displays his authority by staring at his fellow pack members. The subordinate wolves usually look away.

17

Always Alert

Although wolves like lying about relaxing in the sun, they're always alert, watching out for danger or a possible meal.

Luckily wolves have super senses to help them. Like a dog, a wolf has good hearing and can hear high-pitched sounds that are out of the range of people's hearing. If another pack of wolves is howling many miles away, a wolf hears every howl and knows where it's coming from. To do this, a wolf swivels its ears around until it has found the source of the sound.

The wolf also has a keen sense of smell to help it sniff out prey, and good eyesight to catch any nearby movement that may signal danger or food.

A wolf has very keen hearing and can detect sounds up to 6 miles (10 kilometers) away.

18

Wolf Talk

When you talk to your friends, you speak words out loud. But wolves can "talk" to each other without making a sound. When a wolf's ears point straight up and its teeth are bared, it's warning others, "Watch out!" When the pupils of its eyes become narrow slits and its ears are flattened against its head, it's saying, "What's going on here?"

"I'm in charge."

A wolf uses its tail to send messages, too. A tail held high tells other wolves, "I'm in charge here." When a wolf tucks its tail between its legs, it's saying, "I won't argue!"

It's easy to tell when a wolf is happy. It tilts its head and wiggles its body from side to side.

"You're the boss."

All members of a wolf pack recognize these different silent messages. But when they want to have a long-distance conversation with another pack, there's nothing like a good loud howl for keeping in touch!

Ears can "say" a lot! When pack members meet, a dominant wolf shows its superior rank by pointing its ears up. A subordinate wolf turns down its ears.

21

A Howling Good Time

Wolves seem to enjoy howling. Sometimes they howl to gather their pack together before a hunt or to let another wolf pack know they're nearby. But at other times they gather close to each other and wag their tails and seem to howl just for the fun of it.

Once you've heard a wolf howling you'll probably never forget the sound. And when several wolves howl together, they can create the effect of an eerie choir. Some people are frightened by the mysterious and strange sound of a wolf's howl. This fear may contribute to the wolf's bad reputation. But neither the wolf nor its unusual howl present any real threats to humans. In fact, wolves avoid people as much as possible.

Besides howling, wolves make other sounds, too. They bark, yelp, whine, and snarl—just like a dog.

Wolves are well known for their howling, which they do mostly at night. Long and sad-toned, the howl can sound eerie to some people.

No Trespassing!

Home for the wolf pack may be a huge area, anywhere from 40 to 1,000 square miles (100 to 2,500 square kilometers). That's about equal to a large square of land 10 to 16 miles on each side. The pack hunts in this *territory,* or area where it lives, and defends it against wolves from other packs. Occasionally, however, packs do join together for winter hunting.

A wolf pack follows the same hunting routes over and over again. Trotting along logging roads, wildlife trails, or the bank of a river, the pack is constantly on the lookout for its next meal.

Some days the pack may travel as many as 60 miles (95 kilometers) without finding anything to eat. All along the route the alpha male and female mark the territory by spraying urine on the trees and ground. These scent markings are a sign to other wolves that says, "This territory is taken—so keep out!"

Wolves are always on the lookout—for food and for intruders on their territory.

25

Team Hunters

Wolves are *carnivores,* they eat mainly meat. They sometimes hunt alone for the small animals and birds that make up some of their diet. But usually the pack joins together to hunt a large animal, such as a caribou, elk, or moose.

When this happens, the pack works as a team, sometimes cornering the prey. They may divide into two groups and set up an *ambush,* a surprise attack from a hidden place. But even though wolves are clever hunters, most of their prey are too strong even for a pack of hungry wolves. Sometimes the pack goes for days without food.

Some of the wolf's bad reputation may come from this animal's cleverness in hunting. But often, only sick, injured, or old animals are the targets of wolves. This actually helps the herds of its prey by removing animals that are a burden or spread disease.

Wolves in far-northern areas often have pure white coats.

Hungry as a Wolf

Imagine eating a big turkey all by yourself! A full-grown wolf can eat as much as 20 pounds (9 kilograms) of meat at a time. That's about the amount of meat on a big turkey.

Good manners are important when a pack has made a *kill,* caught an animal for food. Pack leaders usually eat first and take the choice pieces of meat. But even though the alpha male and female dominate at a kill, several members of the pack feed together so long as they keep out of each other's way. The most subordinate animals may be kept from feeding until the rest of the pack is done. Anyone who tries to butt in is met with snarls and barks. The message is clear: "Wait your turn!"

A pack normally stays at a kill until the food is eaten. If hunting is poor, a wolf can live for several weeks without food.

At feeding time, wolves have a definite code of conduct. Offenders are quickly put in their place with a warning growl or a vigorous snarl.

Cold Weather Survivors

If a wolf lives where winters are long and cold, it grows a thick, two-layered coat to keep it warm. Long coarse *guard hairs,* hairs that make up the outer layer of fur, shed rain and snow. A layer of thick, short underfur traps body-warmed air next to the wolf's skin.

The treads on your boots help keep you from slipping on ice. A wolf has similar treads on its feet—strong tufts of hair that grow between its cushiony foot pads. These help grip the ice when the wolf travels across frozen terrain.

Since the wolf is so well equipped to run on ice, an icy crust on top of snow makes hunting big game easier. A wolf is light enough to run across the snow without breaking through the crust. But the prey it is chasing sinks into the deep snow each time it leaps forward. This tires and slows the prey, making it easy to catch.

A thick, two-layered winter coat helps make the season cozy for this Tundra Wolf and all other wolves that live in cold northern regions.

Loyal Mates and Good Parents

Toward the end of winter, the alpha male and alpha female *mate,* or come together to produce young. In a pack it's usually only the strongest pair who become parents. If all of the wolves mated, the pack would become too big.

Naturalists, people who study animals and plants, believe that wolves pair for life. But wolf parents get a lot of help raising their families. Both mother and father—as well as aunts, uncles, cousins, and older brothers and sisters—look after the young. If the mother dies, the father and other pack members raise the pups.

Wolves are caring of each other. In the safety of a pack, a wolf may live to be ten or more years old.

A Cozy Den

Before her pups are born, a mother wolf prepares a birth den. She looks for an underground den, perhaps one that's already been used by a fox or badger. If she can't find a ready-made den, she digs one of her own, usually in the side of a sandy hill.

Digging the den is hard work. First the mother wolf digs a long tunnel—about the length of a car. This tunnel goes in and then slopes up so that rain won't run into it. And it has to be narrow so that bigger animals can't crawl into it. At the end of the tunnel, the mother wolf hollows out a space just big enough for herself and her litter.

Once her den is ready, the mother wolf can rest while awaiting the arrival of her pups.

35

Spring Pups

Wolf pups are born in the spring. Sometimes there are as many as 11 of them in the litter, but usually only 5 or 6.

Newborn pups are very tiny—they weigh only about one pound. They have fine woolly hair that is sooty blue-gray in color, and their eyes are shut. They're quite helpless, so the mother wolf keeps them well hidden in the den. She lets them *nurse,* drink milk from her body, and snuggles them in her warm fur.

For the first two weeks the mother wolf and her babies stay in the den undisturbed. The father, however, does bring food for the mother. In about the third week, the father is greeted by excited pups who stagger out of the den on wobbly legs, their eyes now open. By this time the pups also are growing thicker fur coats, and they start to eat meat, which is provided by the father and other pack members.

Wolf mothers are very affectionate and caring with their young.

Happy Relatives

The birth of pups is a big event for a pack. When the babies arrive, their older brothers and sisters gather around the entrance to the den. When the pups finally make their first appearance outdoors, the whole pack takes turns playing with them. It's as if they're all celebrating the pups' birth.

Wolves seem to love babies. They're affectionate and caring with the new pups. They guard them carefully from eagles, wolverines, and other *predators,* animals that hunt other animals for food. The family also keeps the inexperienced little tots from accidentally running into—Ouch!—prickly porcupines. And when mother goes off to hunt, other pack members stay behind to "pupsit."

Though the new pups are as close as a family can be, you might not even guess that they're brothers and sisters. They all look so different. Some pups are pure black, others are speckled beige, and still others are somewhere in between.

Opposite page: *Members of a wolf pack—including a new litter— aren't always the same color. But they're in complete agreement about one thing: they all love the new arrivals.*

Many Mouths To Feed

Once the pups start eating meat, they need a steady supply of it. All the family members help to feed the babies. The adults bring back meat from a kill in their stomachs. When a pup licks an adult's jaws, the adult brings the food back up into its mouth. Then the adult gives this half-digested food to the pup.

This may not sound very appealing to you, but it makes a lot of sense for wolves. If a wolf had to drag fresh meat back to the den, a scent trail would be left leading straight to the helpless pups. By carrying food home in its stomach, a wolf keeps the location of the den a secret from predators. Also, it's much easier over long distances for a wolf to carry food in its stomach than in its mouth.

At about two months, the pups are moved to a summer home—usually a grassy place in the forest where the pups can romp and play. On moving day, the mother wolf often carries one pup at a time in her mouth, gently gripping each by the loose skin on its neck.

Living and Learning

A wolf pup has a lot to learn before it can become an active member of the pack. After learning its most important lesson—its place in the pack—the next important lesson is learning how to hunt. Playing is an important teacher for the young. The pups play "hide-and-seek" and pounce on twigs and leaves—and sometimes on each other! These playful games teach them how to stalk prey and set up ambushes.

Joining the Hunt

By summer's end, the pups look like small versions of their parents. They're getting better at hunting games and they've learned to obey their elders. If they forget their manners, they get a gentle whack from one of the adults. By fall, the pups leave their summer home and begin to hunt with the rest of the pack.

A playful fight may be fun for two young wolves, but it also teaches them how to hunt and attack prey.

Leaving Home

A winter of hunting with the pack polishes the young wolves' hunting skills. By spring they're quite expert. If their pack is small the young wolves may stay with their parents. If it's large, some will leave and start their own pack. Others will join an established pack.

Wolves Today

Due to conservation efforts, wolves are again occupying some of their former homes. Gray Wolves from Minnesota have expanded into Wisconsin and Michigan. Wolves from Canada have moved into Montana and Washington. And in 1995 wolves were released into central Idaho and Yellowstone National Park in Wyoming. Red wolves have been released into North Carolina and Tennessee in recent years.

Conservation programs that preserve wild areas and protect wolves from illegal killing will help wolves get reestablished in their former homes. Education is important, too. People need to learn that much of the wolf's bad reputation is not based on fact. People need to know that wolves deserve our respect.

Words To Know

Alpha The name for the male and female leaders of a pack.

Ambush A surprise attack from a hidden place.

Carnivore Animal that eats mainly meat.

Conservation Protection and careful use of natural resources.

Den Animal home.

Dominant Of a higher rank.

Guard hairs Long coarse hairs that make up the outer layer of a wolf's coat.

Kill Catching an animal for food. Also the animal that is killed.

Litter Young animals born together.

Mate To come together to produce young.

Naturalist Person who studies animals and plants.

Nurse To drink milk from a mother's body.

Pack A group of as many as 20 wolves, usually related, that live together.

Predator Animal that hunts other animals for food.

Prey An animal hunted by another animal for food.

Pup Name for the young of various animals, including wolves.

Subordinate Of a lower rank.

Territory Area that an animal or group of animals lives in and often defends from other animals of the same kind.

Tundra Flat land in the Arctic where no trees grow.

Underfur Short, dense hair that traps body-warmed air next to an animal's skin.

Index

PHOTO CREDITS

Cover: Stephen J. Krasemann, *Valan Photos.* **Interiors:** *Valan Photos:* Stephen J. Krasemann, 4, 8; Bob Hyland, 23; Dennis Schmidt, 33; Esther Schmidt, 34. */*Tom & Pat Leeson, 7, 15, 45. */Hot Shots:* J.D. Taylor, 12, 20, 29. */Norman R. Lightfoot, 16. */Bill Ivy, 19. / J.D. Taylor, 24. */Lowry Photo,* 26. */Tim Fitzharris, 30, 40. */Tom Stack & Associates:* Thomas Kitchin, 36, 43.

Getting To Know...

Nature's Children

WHALES

Mark Shawver

SCHOLASTIC INC.

New York   Toronto   London   Auckland   Sydney
Mexico City   New Delhi   Hong Kong   Buenos Aires

Facts in Brief

Classification of common North American whales

Class: *Mammalia* (mammals)

Order: *Cetacea* (whales, dolphins, and porpoises)

Suborder: *Mysticeti* (baleen whales)

Odontoceti (toothed whales)

Genus: Species that frequent North American waters fall into 9 genera

Species: 12 species of whales and dolphins are commonly found in the oceans around North America

World distribution. Varies with species.

Habitat. Both coastal waters and open ocean.

Distinctive physical characteristics. Flippers and flat, horizontal tail flukes; one or two blowholes on top of head; body is covered and streamlined by a layer of blubber.

Habits. Vary with species.

Diet. Toothed whales: mostly fish and squid; baleen whales: plankton, krill, and very small fish.

Published by Scholastic Inc.
90 Old Sherman Turnpike, Danbury, Connecticut 06816.

SCHOLASTIC and associated logos are trademarks of Scholastic Inc.

ISBN 0-7172-6698-2   Printed in the U.S.A.

Edited by: Elizabeth Grace Zuraw   *Photo Editor:* Nancy Norton
Photo Rights: Ivy Images   *Cover Design:* Niemand Design

Have you ever wondered . . .

The huge Blue Whale, the largest animal that's ever lived on Earth, has a heart the size of a Volkswagen "Beetle" car. Its main blood vessel is big enough for you to crawl through!

What animal is larger than any other animal on Earth—yet has no teeth? If you guessed the Blue Whale, congratulations! The mighty Blue can weigh as much as 21 African elephants. That's bigger than any dinosaur ever was!

You've probably heard someone talk about having "a whale of a time." That usually means the person had a lot of fun, or a lot of trouble, or a lot of whatever. When you think of a whale, you think of something huge, so it's not surprising that people sometimes use the word when they mean of LOT of anything.

Yet not all whales are big. Some, such as the dolphin and the porpoise, are no bigger than a person. There probably are a lot of things about whales that will surprise and amaze you.

Not a Big Fish

Are whales big fish? No! There's one very big difference between fish and whales: whales *aren't* fish. They're mammals, just like dogs or cats or you. And because whales live in the sea, they're called *marine mammals*.

Mammals are animals that have lungs and breathe air. Just as you have to swim up to the surface for a gulp of air after an underwater dive, so must whales. They swim to the surface from time to time and take in air through *blowholes*, nostrils at the top of a whale's head. Fish don't do this. They take

Lungs extract oxygen from air taken in through blowholes.

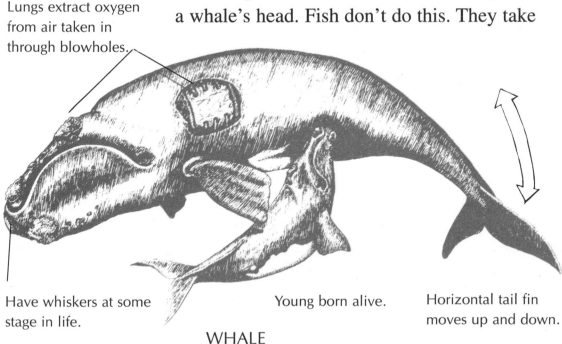

Have whiskers at some stage in life.

Young born alive.

Horizontal tail fin moves up and down.

WHALE

oxygen right from the water through their gills.

Mammals are *warm-blooded.* That means that no matter how cold their surroundings are, their body temperature stays much the same. Mammals are born alive and they *nurse,* drink milk from their mother's body.

Finally, all mammals have hair, at least during one stage of their life. With some marine mammals, such as whales, the hair appears only as whiskers. All whales are born with whiskers, and some keep them all their lives. With most whales, however, the whiskers fall off a few days after they are born.

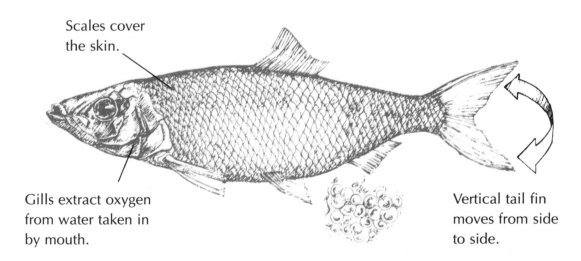

Scales cover the skin.

Gills extract oxygen from water taken in by mouth.

Vertical tail fin moves from side to side.

Young hatch from eggs.

FISH

Once Upon a Time, Long Ago . . .

Many scientists believe that some 70 million years ago, whales lived on land and looked very different. Why did they become water animals?

Perhaps food ran out on land and the hungry ancestors of the whale went to the sea looking for something to eat. Perhaps they stayed in the water to avoid land enemies. But little by little over many generations, their bodies changed so that living in the sea would be easier. For instance, whales developed flippers in place of hands and feet. But a whale's flippers have bones very much like those found in human hands. It seems likely that when whales lived on land, they had hands. As time passed, these hands slowly became flippers that allowed whales to swim better. This is just one of many changes the land whales may have gone through to become sea whales.

Whales were probably smaller when they lived on land. Only animals living in water can grow as big as some whales do because the water supports their enormous body weight.

A Whale of a Family

Whales are not only big in size, they also belong to a big family. There are nearly 80 different kinds of whales—from the small porpoise to the giant Blue Whale.

There are two main types of whales in this whale of a family: whales with teeth and whales without teeth. These two types of whales eat different foods and catch the food in different ways. They are also different in size. In general, toothless whales are large, with the female usually even larger than the male. Toothed whales are smaller in size but a male toothed whale is larger than the female.

Next pages: The whale watchers in this picture would be dwarfed in size if these Killer Whales showed their full length of about 30 feet (9 meters) each.

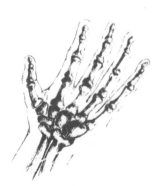

Human hand

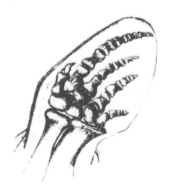

Whale flipper

Notice the similarity between the bones in a whale's flipper and those in a human hand.

9

Whales with Teeth

Toothed whales can be small, like the dolphin and porpoise, or big, like the Sperm Whale.

Small or big, however, toothed whales are dainty eaters—they eat one fish at a time, swallowing it whole. They use their teeth to catch hold of their food, not to chew it.

Toothed whales eat mostly small fish and squid. Some suck food up from the ocean floor, much like a vacuum cleaner sucks up dirt and crumbs. Most often, toothed whales travel and hunt in *pods,* groups of whales that cluster and travel together. Sometimes hundreds of whales travel in one pod and work together to corral or trap fast-moving fish. When people fishing see these pods of whales, they know that a lot of fish probably are nearby.

Killer Whales, also known as Orcas, are toothed whales with big appetites. They hunt fish and many small marine mammals. There are no reliable records, however, of their ever attacking people.

The Toothless Whales

Whales without teeth are called baleen whales. Instead of teeth, they have as many as 400 plates called *baleen* hanging from the roof of their mouth. They use the baleen to strain food out of the water. How?

Baleen whales are gulpers and scoopers. They swim with their mouths open, taking in tons of water full of fish and *plankton,* tiny plants and animals that live in the sea. Then the whales close their mouths and drain the water out through the baleen, where the plankton and fish get trapped. Finally the whale's mighty tongue scoops up the food and the whale swallows it.

Baleen whales are called the great whales because they're so big. Even the smallest of the great whales, the Minke, is about as long as two cars! Would you have guessed that animals that eat such tiny bits of food could grow to be the biggest animals on Earth? Of course, the amounts they eat are huge. A Blue Whale may well eat 9,000 pounds (4,000 kilograms) of food in one day!

Toothless whales such as this Gray Whale have plates of baleen instead of teeth. Also called whalebone, *baleen is made of the same material as your fingernails.*

The Better Not To See You

If you look down at a whale in the water, the dark color on its back blends in with the darker water below. At the same time, if you were underwater and a whale swam above you, its light underside would blend in with the light from above. This type of coloring— dark top and light underside—is called *counter-shading.* Counter-shading makes it harder for a whale's enemies to spot and attack it. The disguise also keeps a whale from being easily seen when it looks for *prey,* animals hunted by other animals for food.

Baleen whales' bodies are usually light gray to brown or black on top with a lighter underside. But toothed whales range in color from the pure white Beluga Whale to the coal black Pilot Whale. Yet most of them, too, are gray with a lighter underside.

This Humpback's graceful leap reveals its counter-shading. A dark top and light underside help disguise a swimming whale.

Coming Up for Air

Opposite page: *Since the Beluga is the only pure white whale in the world, it's often called the White Whale. In fact,* beluga *means "white one" in Russian.*

A whale can't breathe through its mouth as you do. It gets air by breathing through blowholes, the openings at the top of its head. Toothed whales have a single blowhole; baleen whales have two. The blowholes act like a nose. And because they're at the top of its head, a whale can breathe without sticking its whole head out of the water.

As the whale's head comes up for air, the nostrils in its blowholes open and let out the used air in a "cough." The whooshing sound of the air being let out can be heard far away. Then new air is taken in, the nostrils shut, and the whale's head slides back into the water. Each breath takes only one or two seconds.

A whale would drown if it didn't come up for air from time to time. To allow for frequent trips to the water's surface, whales take short "catnaps" many times a day instead of sleeping for long periods at a time.

Spotting a Spout

When whales let their breath out through their blowholes, the effect looks like a spout of water spray.

A whale's spout is not composed of water. It's air that becomes visible when the water vapor in it condenses—just as your breath does on a cold day.

You can often tell one type of whale from another by its spout. The Gray Whale sends out a short bushy spray. The Sperm Whale shoots out its air at an angle. The Blue Whale has a tall skinny spout. And the Right Whale's spout is a bushy "V" that blends to look like a heart!

Opposite page:
Like all Killer Whales this one has a single spout. Highly intellegent creatures, Killer Whales are popular performers in many oceanarium shows.

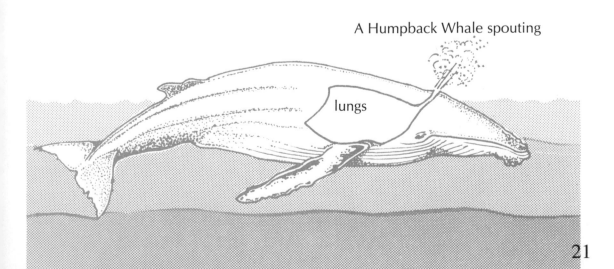

A Humpback Whale spouting

lungs

21

Sights and Sounds

What is it like when you open your eyes underwater? Doesn't everything look blurry? For a whale, it's just the opposite. Whales can see quite well underwater. But above the surface, in air, they can't see well at all!

However, even underwater, whales can't see far; it is often too dark and murky. Whales, therefore, depend a lot on their keen sense of hearing. Sound travels faster in water than in air, so whales can hear sounds quickly and often from a long way off.

Toothed whales can even "see" with sound! They make clicking noises that sound like a very fast typewriter or a high whistle. Then they wait for the echo of these clicks to bounce off an object and come back. The time between sending and receiving the clicks tells the whale how far away an object is. The whale can also tell the object's size and shape

This process is called *echolocation*. Scientists have shown how this works by placing small rubber cups over a dolphin's eyes so that it couldn't see. Then they sent the dolphin out to swim through a maze of hoops. The blindfolded dolphin swam through perfectly every time!

Coming to Their Senses

Since whales spend so little time in air, they seem to have lost the sense of smell. (It isn't possible to smell things underwater.) Instead they have a well-developed sense of taste. Whales in oceanariums are so sensitive to tastes that they refuse food if it has gone even slightly bad.

Echolocation

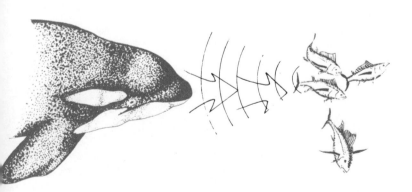

The whale sends out a series of clicking sounds, sometimes as many as 400 per second. When the sounds reach an object, they bounce off and echo back. The timing of the returning clicks tells the whale a great deal about the nature and location of the object.

23

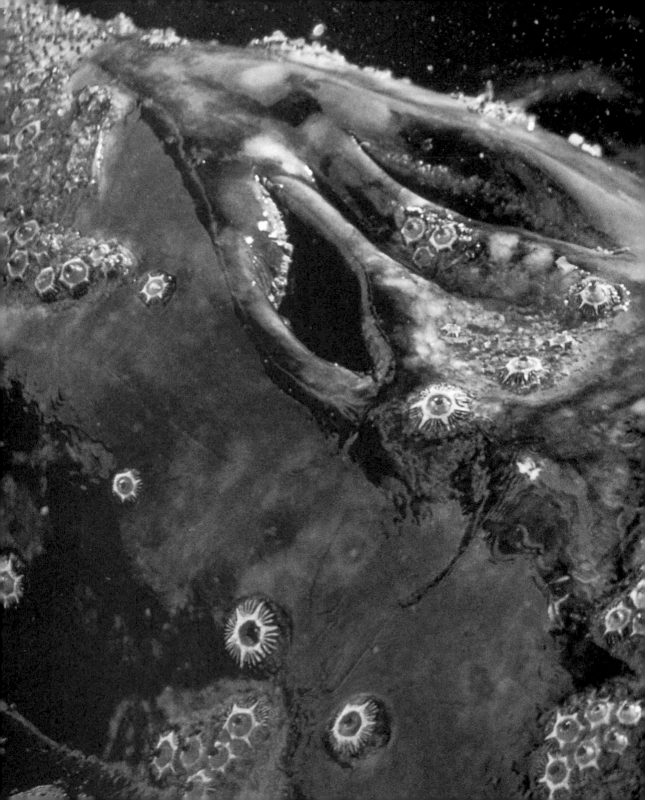

Super Swimmers and Deep Divers

Whales are expert swimmers. They glide through the water by moving their horizontal tail flukes up and down. The flukes are very strong, and some whales can swim very fast. The paddle-like pectoral flippers—the "arms" on either side of a whale's body—are sometimes used when turning. The dorsal fin found on the back of most whales helps them to keep steady in the water.

Whales can make long, deep dives into the ocean. To help them do this, they can slow down their heartbeat so that their air supply lasts longer. During a dive, blood goes only to the most important parts of the whale's body— its brain, heart, and lungs. Also, a whale's blood carries more oxygen than that of most other animals.

Toothed whales are good divers because they must often dive deep to catch their food. Baleen whales usually dive down only to about 500 feet (150 meters). They take a few short, shallow dives, then one long dive that may last for half an hour.

Opposite page:
Notice the barnacles on this Gray Whale's head and blowholes. A single whale may have as much as half a ton (900 kilograms) of barnacles attached to its whole body!

Nature's Loudest Songs

Whales can make a great variety of sounds, including screams, squeaks, and moans. But perhaps the whale most famous for its voice is the Humpback.

Humpbacks are known for their singing. Their songs are among the longest and loudest sounds heard in nature. Some may last for 30 minutes and can be heard over great distances. Until recently, scientists were not sure how whales make these sounds or what they mean. Now many people believe the sounds are the way whales talk to each other.

Humpback songs are sung especially during *mating season,* the time when animals come together to produce young. In effect, these remarkable and haunting sounds are whale love songs.

Humpback Whales, such as those shown here, are famous for their singing. The songs are sung only by males.

The Long Journey

A whale may travel thousands of miles each year. Some whales roam the oceans freely, but most travel within a certain large area—feeding in one place, and mating and giving birth in another. Whales usually feed in cold northern waters and swim to warm southern waters to have their babies. This journey is called *migration.*

One baleen whale, the Gray Whale, has the longest migration of any mammal in the world—about 4,000 miles (6,500 kilometers)! Each year, some of these whales spend summers off the coast of Alaska, then they travel south and spend the winter off the coast of Mexico. Sometimes the journey south takes as long as three months.

Species of whales most commonly found
in North American waters (illustration on next page)

Beluga Whale. A toothed whale that is pure white when fully grown. Found mainly in shallow Arctic waters.

Blue Whale. A baleen whale that weighs about 180,000 pounds (80,000 kilograms). The largest of all whales.

Bottlenose Dolphin. A small toothed whale usually found in warmer waters. The star of many oceanarium shows.

Bowhead Whale. A large baleen whale whose baleen is about 14 feet (4 meters) long. Its baleen is the longest of any whale's.

Fin or **Finback Whale.** The fastest of the baleen whales, it swims 20 miles (30 kilometers) per hour. Prefers deep waters.

Gray Whale. Fairly large baleen whale that spends a lot of time near shore. In recent years some have become quite friendly to people on whale-watching boats.

Humpback Whale. A baleen whale that has very large flippers measuring up to 16 feet (5 meters) in length. It is the most active of the baleen whales.

Killer Whale or **Orca.** A toothed whale that grows to about 30 feet (9 meters). It is known for its intelligence—and for its big appetite. It often performs in oceanarium shows.

Narwhal. A toothed whale, the male of which (and very occasionally, the female) has an external tusk that may reach a length of 10 feet (3 meters).

Minke Whale. The smallest of the baleen whales, the Minke appears to eat fish more often than any other baleen whale.

Right Whale. In early whaling days, this baleen whale was considered the "right" one to hunt because it's such a slow swimmer, making it easy to catch.

Sperm Whale. The largest of the toothed whales and the deepest diver in the ocean. May dive down more than 2 miles (3 kilometers).

KILLER WHALES

FIN WHALE

BOWHEAD

BELUGA

GRAY WHALE

BOTTLENOSE DOLPHINS

SPERM WHALE

HUMPBACK

MINKE WHALES

NARWHAL

E WHALE

RIGHT WHALE

Blanket of Blubber

Gray Whales and some other kinds of whales spend the summer months in the cold waters of the North because food is plentiful there. The whales eat huge amounts and store some of what they eat in a thick layer of fat called *blubber.* This layer of blubber acts like a thick winter coat. It keeps in the whale's body heat and keeps out the cold.

In the early winter, when ice begins to form on the water and there is not as much food available, the whales begin to swim south. During their journey they don't stop to eat or even to rest.

Some whales, such as the Beluga, Bowhead, and Narwhal, stay in the colder waters of the Arctic all year round. When food is scarce in the winter, they absorb the fat stored in their blubber to give them energy.

These Bowhead Whales are swimming about their icy native waters—but the cold doesn't bother them. They have a layer of blubber that's more than 2 feet (half a meter) thick!

All in the Family

Most whales are ready to *mate,* to come together to produce young, when they are about six years old. Whales are choosy about selecting a partner, and sometimes two males will fight over a female. But once a male and female come together, they are very affectionate. Some whales may stay together for life.

During mating season, whales play together, jumping and splashing about and hugging each other with their flippers. They gently roll together, nuzzle, and make sounds to each other.

Whales swim and splash playfully during mating season. Humpbacks, the whales shown here, are also known to make spectactular leaps together out of the water, and to use their long flippers to hug each other.

A Warm Water Cradle

Females usually give birth to one baby, called a *calf,* every two or three years. Since a baby whale does not have a thick layer of blubber to keep it warm, it's best for it to be born in warm water.

Some whale babies, such as those of the Gray Whale and the Humpback, are born in warm lagoons and shallow inlets. There they are safe from the cold, crashing waves of the ocean and safe from enemies, such as sharks and Killer Whales, who sometimes attack calves.

Narwhals and other whales that don't migrate to warmer waters simply move closer to the shore during the arctic summer to have their calves.

Welcome to the family! This baby Humpback, like all whales, has a family name. It's cetacean *(see-TAY-shun), the scientific name for all whales, dolphins, and porpoises. The name comes from the Latin word for "large sea animal."*

A Big Beautiful Baby

A baby whale is huge. A newborn Blue Whale for example, may weigh 4,400 pounds (2,000 kilograms) and be as long as two cars!

Although baby whales are born underwater, they don't stay there long. They cannot breathe underwater. As soon as her baby is born, the mother quickly helps it to the surface for its first breath of air. She does this by pushing and guiding the baby with her snout and flippers. Other female whales may help, too.

A newborn whale is a very hungry baby! It nuzzles close to its mother, nursing from her body. A baby Blue can drink what would equal almost 600 cartons of milk a day! The milk is very rich, and the calf grows quickly.

The baby whale stays close to its mother, who will do anything to keep her baby from harm. If danger is near, a mother whale can become quite fierce.

A baby whale keeps up with its mother by staying close to her side. The water passing between their two bodies actually pulls the calf along.

Whale School

One of the first things a mother whale teaches her baby is when to come up for air. The calf learns by imitating its mother's every move. They swim, surface, breathe, and then dive together. Lessons learned, the calf is soon ready to enter the rougher waters of the open ocean.

Unlike a human baby, which is always completely helpless at birth, a newborn whale is well prepared for life in the ocean. But it still needs its mother to teach it how to improve its diving, surfacing, breathing, and swimming skills.

A baleen calf nurses from its mother for six to eight months. Calves of toothed whales usually nurse up to two years. They need more time because they have more to learn about hunting and catching food. Toothed whale calves generally stay close to their mother until she becomes pregnant again. After that, the young whale is pretty much on its own, although it will stay with the pod.

Opposite page:
This Beluga calf, a toothed whale, will stay with its mother for about two years.

A Whale of a Time

Most whales are playful animals, spending hours diving and splashing about. Whales sometimes *breach,* they leap high into the air, then come crashing down on their side with a big splash.

Whales seem to enjoy each other and are curious about the world around them. And many people are curious about whales. Two popular places for viewing whales in the water are the Atlantic Ocean off New England and the Pacific Ocean off California and Mexico. Humpback, Finback, Minke, and Right Whales delight people on whale-watching tours in the North Atlantic. And every year when thousands of Gray Whales migrate from Alaska to the warm lagoons off the coast of Mexico, people on boats there enjoy looking at the Grays. Some of the whales have become very friendly and let the people get close enough to pet them. They may even push a small boat around with their snout or come up under it and lift it gently with their back. Whale watching can be one whale of a good time!

Opposite Page:
After breaching, two whales slide gracefully into the water. Whales may breach just for fun, or possibly to communicate the presence of food or danger.

Gentle Giants

Whales appear to be very caring animals, and there have been many stories of whales helping each other. Some people once saw two adult Gray Whales helping a baby whale that was stuck on a sandbar. The calf was struggling around on the land and crying out. The two adults breached the water, as if looking for the baby. When they spotted it, they swam toward it and slid up on the sandbar. With one whale on either side of the baby, they rocked until the calf was tightly sandwiched between them. Then they rocked together until they all slid off the sandbar into the water!

The Long Trip Back

Many whales stay in the warm breeding waters until spring. Then they are ready to travel north to their summer feeding grounds. The new mothers and babies are the last to begin the long journey. This gives the calves extra time to grow and become stronger for the long swim north.

What lies in the minds of fascinating animals such as this Blue Whale? No one knows for sure. But scientists hope that someday we will learn a great deal more about these intelligent and complex creatures.

Learning about Whales

In recent years, scientists have developed new methods to study whales in the wild without harming them. By approaching whales carefully and peacefully, researchers can observe their behavior from boats. And they can study whales underwater by using special diving equipment. By now, too, photographers have taken exciting close-up photos of most kinds of whales.

We've learned that whales and dolphins have brains as large and complex as our human brains. We've discovered that whales almost always relate to humans in a gentle, peaceful, and friendly way. And more and more people around the world are experiencing the thrill of going out in boats to watch whales.

Seeing and learning about whales has made people want to preserve them. And whales need protection from some groups that hunt them. These fascinating marine creatures are a special part of nature's world. There is much we don't yet know about whales, but if we take good care of them and their water world, who knows what great future discoveries we may make.

Words To Know

Baleen   Plates in the upper jaw of some whales that strain out the small animals the whale eats.

Blowhole   Nostril at the top of a whale's head through which it breathes. Baleen whales have two blowholes.

Blubber   A layer of fat under the skin of most marine mammals.

Breach   To leap out of the water.

Breed   To come together to produce young.

Calf   Whale baby.

Counter-shading   The coloring of a whale that helps to make it less noticeable.

Echolocation   Method used by some whales to find their way underwater by sending out sounds and listening to the returning echoes.

Fluke   One of the two sections making up a whale's horizontal tail.

Krill   Small shrimp-like animals.

Mammal   Warm-blooded animal that breathes air, is born alive, drinks its mother's milk, and has hair at some stage of its life.

Marine mammal   Mammal that lives in the sea.

Mate   To come together to produce young.

Mating Season   The time of year during which animals mate.

Migration   Travel from one region to another for feeding or breeding.

Nurse   To drink milk from a mother's body.

Plankton   Tiny animals and plants that live in the sea.

Prey   Animal hunted by another animal for food.

Pod   A group of marine mammals that cluster and travel together.

Warm-blooded   Having the same body temperature regardless of the surrounding temperature.

Index

PHOTO CREDITS
Cover: Jim Nahmens, *EarthViews*. **Interiors:** Doc White, 4, 34, 45. /*Tom Stack & Associates:* Thomas
Kitchin, 10-11; Jeff Foott, 12; Dave B. Fleetham, 38. /*EarthViews:* Thomas Johnson, 15; Jim Nahmens, 16;
Alan J. Cortash, 24; Stephen Leatherwood, 33; James D. Watt, 37. /Fred Bruemmer, 19, 41. /*Valan Photos:*
Esther Schmidt, 20; R. Galbraith, 27. /*Bio-Tec Images:* George D. Lepp, 42.
All art illustrations: Jenniffer Julich and Jeannette McNaughton.